Her Presence Still Speaks

Honoring the Power, Influence, and Legacy of a

Mother

Ethan L. Ketterer

Her Presence Still Speaks
Honoring the Power, Influence, and Legacy of a Mother

Scripture quotations are taken from the **King James Version (KJV)** of the Holy Bible.

This book is a work of reflection and encouragement. The experiences and examples shared are intended to inspire and uplift and are not a substitute for professional, legal, or medical advice.

Published by:
KTURN Publishing
Making a Turn for the Better

For information about books, workshops, conferences, and speaking engagements, please contact:
admin1@mykturn.com

ISBN (Paperback): 978-8-9999942-3-3

HER PRESENCE STILL SPEAKS

To my mother—

whose presence spoke louder than words,

whose sacrifices laid foundations unseen,

and whose love continues to echo

through every life she touched.

This book is because of you.

III

Acknowledgements

This book exists because of presence—seen and unseen, spoken and silent.

First, I give honor to God, whose wisdom, grace, and guidance continue to shape my life and calling. Without His covering, direction, and patience, these pages would not exist.

I acknowledge my mother. Your presence, sacrifices, prayers, and unwavering love laid a foundation that continues to guide my life. In moments when words were few and circumstances were heavy, your consistency spoke louder than instruction. What you carried, what you endured, and what you poured out did not go unnoticed. This book is, in many ways, a reflection of the impact of your presence.

I also acknowledge the mothers—biological, spiritual, adoptive, and chosen—whose sacrifices are often unseen but never without impact. Your prayers, perseverance, and quiet strength have shaped generations in ways words can barely capture.

To the women who stood in the gap, nurtured when it was inconvenient, corrected with love, and remained present when walking away would have been easier—thank you. Your presence mattered more than you may ever realize.

To my wife, thank you for your continued support, encouragement, and understanding during the moments when writing required time, focus, and sacrifice. Your belief in this work made room for it to come to life.

To every reader who has ever felt the lasting impact of a woman's presence—whether through guidance, prayer, protection, or love—this book is for you. May these pages remind you that what she gave mattered, what she carried counted, and her presence made a difference.

Introduction

Presence is often misunderstood. It is easy to measure presence by physical nearness—by attendance, proximity, or visibility. Yet the kind of presence that truly shapes lives cannot be reduced to location alone. True presence is revealed through consistency, sacrifice, guidance, prayer, correction, protection, and love. It is presence that remains steady when circumstances shift and influence that lingers long after a moment has passed.

This book was written to honor that kind of presence.

Because of her presence, lessons were learned without formal instruction. Because of her presence, strength was built in quiet moments. Because of her presence, stability was found during seasons of uncertainty. Long before accomplishments were recognized or milestones were celebrated, there was a woman whose influence quietly shaped the journey.

Too often, the labor of mothers and maternal figures is carried out without applause or acknowledgment. They nurture through exhaustion, lead through uncertainty, and remain steadfast when life demands more than they feel they have to give. Their presence fills gaps that others never see and answers prayers that are never spoken aloud. Even when their efforts are unseen or misunderstood, the impact remains undeniable.

This book is not written to idealize perfection, but to honor faithfulness. It recognizes the mothers who showed up despite limitations, the women who stood in the gap when others stepped away, and the maternal figures who loved without condition. It acknowledges biological mothers, spiritual mothers, guardians, mentors, and women who carried responsibility that was never formally assigned to them.

Presence takes many forms. Sometimes it is guidance offered at the right moment. Sometimes it is correction given with love. Sometimes it is protection provided quietly, without recognition. At other times, presence simply looks like staying—remaining committed when it would be easier to retreat. Each of these expressions leaves a lasting imprint on the lives they touch.

You may be reading these pages as a mother reflecting on your own journey, wondering whether the sacrifices you made truly mattered. You may be a daughter or son beginning to understand the depth of influence a woman had on your life. Or you may be someone who was shaped by a maternal presence that was not biological, but no less significant. Wherever you find yourself, this book invites you to pause and reflect on the power of presence and the legacy it creates.

Each chapter explores a different dimension of presence—strength, sacrifice, endurance, faith, and legacy. Scripture and reflection are woven throughout to encourage thoughtful engagement, prayerful consideration, and personal application. This is not a book meant to be rushed, but one designed to be experienced slowly, allowing space for remembrance, gratitude, and growth.

If you have ever questioned whether your presence made a difference, these pages serve as a reminder that it did. If you have ever benefited from the steady influence of a woman who stayed when it would have been easier to leave, this book is an invitation to honor that gift.

Because of her presence, lives were shaped.
Because of her presence, purpose was nurtured.
Because of her presence, foundations were built that still stand today.

Closing Scripture (KJV)

"Her children arise up, and call her blessed; her husband also, and he praiseth her."

— Proverbs 31:28 (KJV)

TABLE OF CONTENTS

Chapter 1

Presence That Shapes Identity

"Train up a child in the way he should go: and when he is old, he will not depart from it."
— **Proverbs 22:6 (KJV)**

Identity is not formed in a single moment. It is shaped over time—through repeated exposure, consistent guidance, and steady presence. Long before a person understands who they are becoming, they are absorbing what they see, hear, and experience. Presence plays a powerful role in that process.

A mother's presence often becomes the first mirror through which a child sees the world and themselves. In the way she speaks, corrects, comforts, and carries responsibility, identity begins to take root. Even when she does not realize it, her presence sends messages that settle deeply: *You are valued. You are seen. You matter.*

Training a child is not limited to instruction alone. Proverbs 22:6 does not suggest a single lesson or conversation, but a way—a path shaped by repetition, example, and direction. That path is carved through presence. It is the daily showing up, the consistent guidance, and the unwavering care that quietly mold character and confidence.

Many of the most influential lessons are never spoken aloud. They are demonstrated. Children learn resilience by watching how challenges are handled. They learn compassion by observing how others are treated. They learn perseverance by seeing someone continue even when circumstances are heavy. Presence teaches before words ever do.

A mother's presence helps answer questions a child may not yet know how to ask. *Who am I? Am I safe? Do I belong?* The answers are often delivered not through speeches, but through consistency—being there when it would be easier not to be, listening when time is limited, and remaining steady when emotions are high.

Identity is shaped in both ordinary and extraordinary moments. In routine days filled with responsibilities, presence creates stability. In moments of uncertainty or transition, presence provides grounding. Over time, those moments accumulate, forming a foundation that supports confidence, self-worth, and purpose.

This shaping does not require perfection. No mother carries out her role flawlessly. Yet identity is not built on perfection; it is built on faithfulness. Children remember who stayed, who tried, and who remained engaged—even when circumstances were imperfect. Presence does not erase hardship, but it helps a child navigate it.

As children grow, the influence of early presence continues to echo. The words spoken, the values modeled, and the love demonstrated become internal guideposts. Even when distance grows and seasons change, the imprint remains. Identity formed through presence does not disappear with time—it matures.

For some, this chapter may stir gratitude. For others, it may surface reflection or longing. Some were shaped by consistent presence, while others experienced absence or inconsistency. Still, the truth remains: presence has power. When offered faithfully, it shapes identity in ways that extend far beyond childhood.

This chapter invites reflection not only on the presence received, but on the presence given. Whether you are a mother, mentor, guardian, or influential figure, your presence is shaping someone's understanding of themselves. What you model, what you prioritize, and how you respond matters more than you may ever realize.

Presence does not require grand gestures. It requires intention. It requires showing up repeatedly, offering guidance patiently, and remaining available emotionally and spiritually. Over time, that presence becomes a voice that continues to speak—long after the moment has passed.

Because of her presence, identity was formed.
Because of her presence, confidence took root.
Because of her presence, a foundation was laid that continues to stand.

Chapter 1 Reflection Page

Reflect

Presence shapes identity long before identity is understood. Take a moment to pause and reflect on how presence—consistent, loving, or even inconsistent—has influenced your life.

1. Who were the primary figures whose presence shaped your early sense of identity?
    (Mother, guardian, mentor, spiritual influence, or other)

2. What messages did their presence communicate to you about who you are?
    (Consider words spoken, actions modeled, or moments remembered.)

3. In what ways do you still see the influence of that presence in your decisions, confidence, or values today?

Apply & Pray

Reflection becomes transformation when it leads to intention and action.

4. How are you currently offering presence to others? *(Children, family members, students, coworkers, or those you lead.)*

5. What does "faithful presence" look like in your current season of life?

Prayer Prompt

Take a moment to pray over the influence of presence—both given and received.

Lord, thank You for the presence that helped shape my identity. Where my foundation is strong, help me to honor it. Where there were gaps, help me to heal and grow. Teach me to be present with intention, faithfulness, and love, so that my presence may speak life into others. Amen.

Chapter 2

The Power of Staying

"And let us not be weary in well doing: for in due season we shall reap, if we faint not."
— **Galatians 6:9 (KJV)**

Staying does not always look powerful. Often, it looks ordinary. It looks like showing up again after a long day. It looks like choosing consistency when recognition is absent. It looks like remaining committed when leaving would feel easier. Yet staying carries a power that time eventually reveals.

The power of staying is not found in dramatic moments, but in repeated ones. It is built through faithfulness—through decisions made daily to remain present, engaged, and invested. Many lives are shaped not by extraordinary gestures, but by someone who simply refused to walk away.

Mothers and maternal figures understand this power deeply. Staying is woven into their role. They stay through uncertainty, exhaustion, misunderstanding, and seasons where progress feels invisible. They stay when gratitude is delayed and when results are not immediately evident. Their presence becomes a stabilizing force in lives that are still forming.

Galatians 6:9 speaks directly to this reality. It acknowledges weariness without condemning it. The verse does not deny fatigue; it addresses it. It offers a promise that perseverance carries reward, even when the outcome is delayed. Staying, when done in faith, is never wasted.

There are moments when staying feels costly. It requires patience when patience is thin. It demands grace when appreciation is lacking. It asks for endurance when strength feels depleted. Yet the power of staying lies in what it produces over time—security, trust, and growth that cannot be rushed.

Children, families, and communities learn safety through consistency. Knowing someone will remain present provides grounding in uncertain seasons. Staying communicates a message deeper than words: *You are worth my time. You are worth my effort. You are worth my commitment.*

Staying does not mean ignoring personal limits or enduring harm. It means choosing faithfulness within wisdom. It means remaining engaged where God has placed you, trusting that your consistency is doing work you may not yet see. Presence paired with endurance creates an environment where growth can take root.

Many who reflect back on their lives recognize that the people who shaped them most were not always the loudest or most visible, but the most consistent. They were the ones who stayed—through transitions, mistakes, and moments of doubt. Their presence became an anchor when everything else felt unstable.

This chapter invites reflection on the moments when staying felt heavy and the times when perseverance seemed unnoticed. It also encourages recognition of the unseen harvest being cultivated through faithful presence. Growth often happens quietly, beneath the surface, long before it becomes visible.

If you are in a season where staying feels difficult, let this chapter serve as reassurance. Weariness does not negate purpose. Fatigue does not cancel faithfulness. The power of staying is not measured by immediate results, but by long-term impact.

Because of her staying, stability was formed.
Because of her staying, trust was built.
Because of her staying, lives were strengthened in ways that continue to endure.

Chapter 2 Reflection Page

Reflect

Staying requires faith, patience, and commitment—especially when results are not immediate. Take time to consider the role of endurance and consistency in your own life.

1. Who has stayed in your life during difficult or uncertain seasons?
   (Consider mothers, mentors, spiritual leaders, or others who remained present.)

2. What impact did their consistency have on your sense of stability, trust, or growth?

3. Can you recall a season when staying felt heavy or unappreciated? What helped you endure?

Apply & Pray

Endurance becomes meaningful when it is anchored in purpose and guided by faith.

4. In what areas of your life is God calling you to remain faithful, even when feels slow progress?

5. How can you practice healthy, intentional staying— remaining present without neglecting wisdom or self-care?

Prayer Prompt

Pause and invite God to strengthen you in seasons that require perseverance.

Lord, help me not to grow weary in well doing. When staying feels heavy, remind me of the purpose behind my faithfulness. Strengthen me to remain present with wisdom, patience, and grace, trusting that you are working even when I cannot see the results. Amen.

Chapter 3

Lessons Taught Without Words

"Be ye followers of me, even as I also am of Christ."
— 1 Corinthians 11:1 (KJV)

Some of the most powerful lessons are never spoken. They are lived. They are modeled quietly through choices, reactions, priorities, and perseverance. Long before instruction is understood, observation is absorbed. Presence teaches without words.

Mothers and maternal figures often instruct without realizing it. In how they handle pressure, respond to disappointment, or extend grace, they communicate values that settle deeply. Children watch how love is expressed, how faith is practiced, and how adversity is navigated. These daily demonstrations become lessons that last.

Scripture affirms the power of example. In 1 Corinthians 11:1, Paul invites others to follow him as he follows Christ. The call is not rooted in perfect speech or flawless behavior, but in visible alignment. Faith becomes credible when it is seen in action. Presence gives integrity to instruction.

Words can inform, but example shapes belief. A child may forget what was said, but will remember what was done. They remember tone, consistency, and response. They remember who remained calm, who offered patience, and who chose grace when emotions were high. These unspoken lessons form a framework for decision-making long after childhood.

Lessons taught without words are often revealed over time. A mother's consistent prayer life, her discipline wrapped in love, her resilience in hardship—all become reference points later in life. When faced with choices, individuals often draw from what they observed rather than what they were told.

This kind of teaching requires authenticity. Children are perceptive. They notice inconsistencies between words and actions. Presence that aligns behavior with belief builds trust. When faith, character, and conduct are consistent, lessons carry weight without explanation.

Teaching through presence does not require perfection. It requires honesty. Admitting mistakes, seeking forgiveness, and demonstrating growth all communicate powerful lessons. Children learn that strength includes humility and that faith includes perseverance through failure.

Many who reflect on their upbringing recognize that their strongest lessons came from watching how someone lived. They learned integrity by observing fairness. They learned compassion by witnessing empathy. They learned perseverance by seeing endurance practiced daily.

This chapter invites reflection on both sides of influence. It encourages recognition of the lessons absorbed through observation and challenges readers to consider the lessons they are currently modeling. Whether intentional or not, presence is always teaching.

The influence of lived example does not fade with time. Long after conversations are forgotten, the image of consistency remains. Presence continues to speak through the lessons it modeled—quietly, steadily, and faithfully.

Because of her example, faith was made visible.
Because of her actions, values took shape.

Because of her presence, lessons were taught without words.

Chapter 3 Reflection Page

Reflect

Many of the most lasting lessons are learned through observation rather than instruction. Take time to reflect on the examples that shaped you.

1. Who modeled values, faith, or character for you without needing to explain them?
    (Consider mothers, caregivers, mentors, or other influential figures.)

2. What behaviors or attitudes did you observe that later influenced your own choices or beliefs?

3. How did consistency—or inconsistency—between words and actions affect your trust or understanding?

Apply & Pray

Presence is always teaching, whether intentionally or unintentionally.

4. What lessons might others be learning from how you respond to challenges, pressure, or disappointment?

5. In what ways can you more intentionally model faith, patience, and integrity in your daily life?

Prayer Prompt

Invite God to align your example with your values and faith.

Lord, help me to live in a way that reflects Your truth, even when words are not spoken. Align my actions with my faith, and let my presence teach lessons that lead others toward integrity, grace, and wisdom. Amen.

Chapter 4

Carrying More Than We Knew

"He shall feed his flock like a shepherd: he shall gather the lambs with his arm, and carry them in his bosom, and shall gently lead those that are with young."
— **Isaiah 40:11 (KJV)**

Much of what a mother carries is unseen. While the visible responsibilities of caregiving are often acknowledged, the invisible weight—the emotional, mental, and spiritual load—frequently goes unnoticed. Yet it is this unseen burden that shapes presence most profoundly.

Mothers carry concern before it becomes crisis. They anticipate needs, absorb worries, and shoulder responsibility quietly. Long before a child is aware of difficulty, a mother is often already navigating solutions, praying through uncertainty, and adjusting her own strength to provide stability.

Isaiah 40:11 offers a tender image of care—one that acknowledges both gentleness and weight. To carry is not passive; it is intentional. It requires strength paired with compassion. In the same way, mothers often balance tenderness with endurance, offering comfort while managing pressure behind the scenes.

Carrying more than we knew means holding emotional weight without complaint. It means making space for others while minimizing personal strain. Mothers often carry disappointment privately so that those they love can remain unburdened. Their presence becomes a place of refuge, even when their own reserves feel depleted.

Many do not realize the cost of this carrying until much later. Only with time does the depth of sacrifice become clear. What once felt effortless is later recognized as intentional strength. What seemed ordinary is revealed as extraordinary endurance.

Carrying also includes navigating seasons of uncertainty. Mothers carry fear when outcomes are unclear. They carry hope when circumstances feel fragile. They carry faith when answers are delayed. Often, they carry these things alone, trusting God to supply what they cannot.

This chapter is not written to romanticize exhaustion, but to honor faithfulness. Carrying weight does not mean ignoring personal limits. It means stewarding responsibility with wisdom, grace, and reliance on God. Even strength must be replenished.

For some readers, this chapter may awaken gratitude. For others, it may uncover unacknowledged labor—both given and received. Recognizing what was carried creates space for appreciation, healing, and rest.

Presence becomes powerful when it bears weight quietly. It shelters others while trusting God for renewal. It reflects strength that does not demand recognition, but leaves a lasting imprint nonetheless.

Because of her carrying, others felt safe.
Because of her carrying, burdens were lightened.
Because of her carrying, strength was quietly multiplied.

Chapter 4 Reflection Page

Reflect

Much of what is carried in love is unseen. Take time to reflect on the weight that was carried—by others and by yourself.

1. Who in your life carried more than you realized at the time?
   (Consider emotional, spiritual, or practical burdens.)

2. What responsibilities or concerns did they quietly shoulder to create stability or peace for others?

3. When did you begin to recognize the depth of what was carried on your behalf?

Apply & Pray

Recognizing unseen weight creates space for gratitude, healing, and healthier boundaries.

4. In what areas of your life are you currently carrying weight quietly?
   (Consider emotional, spiritual, or relational burdens.)

5. What steps can you take to release, share, or steward that weight with wisdom and faith?

Prayer Prompt

Pause and offer your burdens to God, trusting Him as the ultimate source of strength.

Lord, You see the weight that is carried quietly. Thank You for those who bore burdens in love and faith. Where I am carrying more than I should, help me to release what is not mine to hold and to trust You for strength, renewal, and rest. Amen.

Chapter 5

Strength Built in Quiet Places

"God is in the midst of her; she shall not be moved: God shall help her, and that right early."
— Psalm 46:5 (KJV)

Strength is often associated with visibility—being seen, recognized, or applauded. Yet some of the deepest strength is developed far from the spotlight. It is formed in quiet places where faith is tested privately and endurance is built without acknowledgment.

Mothers and maternal figures frequently develop strength in these unseen spaces. In moments of solitude, prayer, and silent perseverance, they draw on faith that sustains them when external support is limited. Their strength is not loud, but it is steady.

Psalm 46:5 offers reassurance that strength does not depend on surroundings. God's presence within provides stability when circumstances shift. To be "not moved" does not mean untouched by difficulty; it means anchored despite it. Quiet strength is rooted in trust rather than recognition.

Strength built in quiet places often reveals itself when challenges arise. It shows in calm responses during chaos, patience in prolonged uncertainty, and courage when outcomes are unclear. This strength is not reactive—it is grounded.

Quiet places include early mornings filled with prayer, late nights marked by reflection, and moments of decision made without counsel. In these spaces, faith is refined. Strength is not borrowed from others but cultivated through reliance on God.

This chapter honors the unseen work that fortifies presence. Mothers often prepare emotionally and spiritually before others are aware of need. Their private endurance becomes public stability. What is built quietly supports others loudly.

Strength built in quiet places also teaches resilience by example. Children and those observing learn that strength does not require constant explanation. They learn that faith can be practiced without performance and endurance without display.

This kind of strength leaves a lasting impression. It teaches others how to remain grounded when circumstances feel unstable. It offers reassurance that unseen faithfulness carries visible fruit in time.

For readers navigating their own quiet places, this chapter serves as encouragement. The work being done in solitude is not wasted. God is present in those moments, shaping strength that will sustain you and others.

Because of her quiet strength, stability was provided. Because of her anchored faith, others were steadied. Because of her trust, strength was built where few could see.

Chapter 5 Reflection — Page One

Reflect

Some of the strongest moments of growth happen in places where no one is watching. Take time to reflect on the quiet spaces that have shaped your strength.

1. What "quiet places" have contributed most to your personal growth or resilience?
    (Moments of prayer, solitude, reflection, or perseverance.)

2. How have those quiet moments prepared you to respond with stability during challenging times?

3. Who modeled quiet strength for you through faith, patience, or endurance?

Apply & Pray

Quiet strength becomes lasting strength when it is nurtured with intention and faith.

4. In what areas of your life are you currently being strengthened through unseen work?

5. How can you protect or prioritize time for quiet renewal in your current season?

Prayer Prompt

Pause and invite God into your quiet spaces.

Lord, thank You for meeting me in the stillness. Strengthen me in places where growth is unseen and faith is quietly formed. Help me to trust that You are present, building stability and endurance that will serve others in due time. Amen.

Chapter 6

Correction Wrapped in Love

"For whom the LORD loveth he correcteth; even as a father the son in whom he delighteth."
— Proverbs 3:12 (KJV)

Correction is often misunderstood. It is frequently associated with punishment rather than care, discipline rather than devotion. Yet correction, when rooted in love, serves as protection. It guides rather than wounds and instructs rather than diminishes.

Mothers and maternal figures understand the delicate balance correction requires. They correct not to control, but to protect. Their guidance is shaped by concern for character, safety, and growth. Even when correction is uncomfortable, its intention is anchored in love.

Proverbs 3:12 reminds us that correction is evidence of care. It is not the absence of love, but a sign of it. Just as God corrects those He delights in, loving correction communicates value. It says, *You matter too much to be left without guidance.*

Correction wrapped in love requires wisdom. It considers timing, tone, and purpose. It seeks to instruct rather than shame. When delivered with patience and compassion, correction builds trust instead of fear. It creates an environment where growth is possible.

Many lessons of right and wrong are learned through loving correction. Boundaries teach safety. Accountability develops responsibility. Discipline offered with clarity and care shapes decision-making long after the moment has passed.

Children often recognize the value of correction later in life. What once felt restrictive is later understood as protective. The guidance that was resisted becomes the wisdom that is remembered. Loving correction leaves an imprint that matures with time.

This chapter also invites reflection on how correction has been received. Some experienced guidance delivered with care, while others encountered correction that lacked compassion. Healing begins by recognizing the difference and choosing healthier patterns moving forward.

Correction wrapped in love does not demand perfection—from the giver or the receiver. It allows room for growth, mistakes, and learning. It models humility by acknowledging that guidance, too, evolves with understanding.

For those offering correction today, this chapter serves as encouragement. Speak truth with gentleness. Guide with patience. Remember that how correction is delivered matters as much as the correction itself.

Because of her loving correction, boundaries were established.
Because of her guidance, wisdom took root.
Because of her love, growth was nurtured with care.

Chapter 6 Reflection Page

Reflect

Correction, when rooted in love, shapes wisdom and character. Take time to reflect on how guidance and boundaries have influenced your growth.

1. Who offered you correction that was clearly motivated by love and care?
   (Consider how it was delivered and how it impacted you.)

2. How did loving correction help shape your decision-making, values, or sense of responsibility?

3. Have you experienced correction that lacked compassion? How has that shaped your understanding of guidance today?

Apply & Pray

Correction offered with wisdom becomes a tool for growth rather than fear.

4. In what areas of your life are boundaries currently serving as protection rather than restriction?

5. How can you offer correction to others in a way that reflects patience, clarity, and love?

Prayer Prompt

Pause and invite God to shape how you give and receive correction.

Lord, help me to receive correction with humility and to offer it with love. Teach me to guide with wisdom, patience, and compassion, so that growth may flourish without fear. Amen.

Chapter 7

Standing in the Gap

"And I sought for a man among them, that should make up the hedge, and stand in the gap before me for the land, that I should not destroy it: but I found none."
— **Ezekiel 22:30 (KJV)**

Standing in the gap is an act of courage. It requires seeing danger before it becomes visible and responding before damage is done. It is the willingness to intervene, to protect, and to advocate when others may remain silent or unaware.

Mothers and maternal figures often stand in the gap instinctively. They recognize shifts in behavior, sense unspoken needs, and respond to threats—emotional, spiritual, or physical—before they fully surface. Their presence becomes a hedge, offering protection where vulnerability exists.

Ezekiel 22:30 highlights the importance of intercession and advocacy. To stand in the gap is to step between harm and those at risk. It is a position of responsibility that demands awareness, prayer, and action. While the verse speaks of the absence of one willing to stand, it underscores the power that presence carries when someone does.

Standing in the gap does not always involve visible confrontation. Often, it looks like quiet advocacy—asking questions, seeking clarity, and creating safe spaces for growth. It may involve prayer offered privately, conversations held thoughtfully, or boundaries established firmly but lovingly.

This form of presence requires discernment. Knowing when to intervene and when to allow growth takes wisdom. Mothers frequently navigate this balance, offering protection without stifling development and guidance without control. Their presence shields while still allowing independence to form.

Many lives are altered because someone chose to stand in the gap. A word spoken at the right time, a boundary enforced, or a prayer lifted can redirect a path. Though these moments may never be publicly acknowledged, their impact can be life-altering.

Standing in the gap also requires endurance. Advocacy is not always welcomed. Protection is not always understood. Yet presence rooted in love persists, trusting that intervention serves を見る a greater purpose.

This chapter invites reflection on the moments when someone stood between you and harm—whether you realized it then or not. It also challenges readers to consider where they are called to stand in the gap today. Presence that protects is presence that speaks powerfully.

Because of her willingness to stand, danger was delayed. Because of her advocacy, paths were redirected. Because of her presence, protection was provided when it mattered most.

Chapter 7 Reflection Page

Reflect

Standing in the gap often happens quietly and without recognition. Take time to reflect on moments of protection and advocacy in your life.

1. Who has stood in the gap for you—interceding, advocating, or protecting you when you were vulnerable or unaware?

2. What actions did they take that helped shield you from harm or redirect your path?

3. When did you later realize the impact of their presence and intervention?

____

____

Apply & Pray

Presence that protects often requires courage, discernment, and obedience.

4. In what areas of your life might God be calling you to stand in the gap for someone else?

____

____

____

5. What fears, hesitations, or obstacles make standing in the gap difficult for you, and how can you bring those honestly before God?

____

____

____

Prayer Prompt

Pause and invite God to guide you in advocacy and intercession.

Lord, thank You for those who stood in the gap on my behalf. Give me discernment to recognize where You are calling me to intervene, protect, and advocate with wisdom and love. Strengthen my courage to stand when it matters most. Amen.

Chapter 8

Faith Passed Hand to Hand

"When I call to remembrance the unfeigned faith that is in thee, which dwelt first in thy grandmother Lois, and thy mother Eunice; and I am persuaded that in thee also."
— 2 Timothy 1:5 (KJV)

Faith is often received before it is understood. It is handed down through example, practice, and presence long before it is articulated in words. For many, faith was first encountered not in a sanctuary, but in the steady life of a woman who lived what she believed.

Mothers and maternal figures frequently become the first teachers of faith. Through prayer, scripture, and daily decisions, they demonstrate belief in tangible ways. Their faith is not always preached, but it is practiced—and that practice leaves an imprint.

Paul's words to Timothy acknowledge this powerful transfer. Faith did not originate in Timothy alone; it was nurtured through generations. The faith that dwelt in his grandmother and mother became a living inheritance. Presence created continuity. Example created trust.

Faith passed hand to hand is rarely dramatic. It is cultivated in ordinary moments—bedtime prayers, early morning devotions, whispered encouragement, and quiet trust during hardship. These moments accumulate, shaping belief systems and spiritual confidence.

This kind of faith is resilient because it is relational. It is reinforced by memory, example, and consistency. When doubt arises, individuals often recall how faith sustained someone they trusted. That memory becomes an anchor.

Not all faith journeys are identical. Some inherit strong spiritual foundations, while others encounter faith later in life through spiritual mothers or mentors. Still, the principle remains: faith grows when it is modeled authentically.

This chapter honors the women whose faith was lived faithfully, even when outcomes were uncertain. Their belief became a covering, offering spiritual stability and direction. Long after words fade, the memory of their faith continues to speak.

Faith passed hand to hand also invites responsibility. Those who have received faith are called to steward it. Presence continues the cycle—teaching, modeling, and nurturing belief in others.

For readers reflecting on their own spiritual lineage, this chapter encourages gratitude and intentionality. Faith is not only something we hold; it is something we pass on through presence and practice.

Because of her faith, belief was nurtured.
Because of her example, trust was strengthened.
Because of her presence, faith continues to speak across generations.

Chapter 8 Reflection Page

Reflect

Faith is often received through presence before it is understood through teaching. Take time to reflect on the spiritual influence that shaped you.

1. Who modeled faith for you in a consistent and authentic way?

   (Mother, grandmother, spiritual mother, mentor, or other influence.)

2. What practices, habits, or moments made their faith visible to you?

   (Prayer, worship, scripture, trust during hardship, encouragement.)

3. How has their example influenced your own faith journey, beliefs, or trust in God?

Apply & Pray

Faith grows when it is lived intentionally and shared faithfully.

4. In what ways are you currently passing faith on to others through your presence and example?

5. What steps can you take to strengthen the spiritual legacy you are building for future generations?

Prayer Prompt

Pause and thank God for the faith you have received and the opportunity to steward it.

Lord, thank You for the faith that was poured into my life through faithful presence. Help me to honor that legacy by living my faith authentically and passing it on with love, consistency, and trust. May my presence continue what You have begun. Amen

.Chapter 9

When Presence Becomes Shelter

"He that dwelleth in the secret place of the most High shall abide under the shadow of the Almighty."
— Psalm 91:1 (KJV)

Shelter is more than physical protection. It is emotional safety, spiritual covering, and the assurance that someone is watching over you. Presence becomes shelter when it creates a space where fear is eased and trust can grow.

Mothers and maternal figures often serve as shelters long before others recognize the need. Their presence absorbs worry, calms uncertainty, and provides reassurance during moments of instability. In their care, chaos is quieted and vulnerability is protected.

Psalm 91:1 describes a dwelling place—an environment of covering and peace. To dwell is to remain. To abide is to stay close. Shelter is not temporary; it is sustained through presence and trust. In the same way, maternal presence creates environments where safety is felt, even when circumstances remain challenging.

Presence becomes shelter through consistency. It shows up during storms and remains steady when pressure increases. It offers refuge without judgment and support without conditions. This kind of presence does not eliminate hardship, but it changes how hardship is experienced.

Shelter also involves awareness. Mothers often sense distress before it is expressed. They notice subtle shifts, unspoken fears, and quiet needs. Their presence responds with protection—sometimes through action, sometimes through silence, and often through prayer.

Many reflect later in life and recognize that what they experienced as safety was not accidental. It was cultivated intentionally. Someone chose to remain present, to provide structure, and to offer reassurance. That shelter shaped resilience and trust.

This chapter invites reflection on the shelters you have known—places of safety created through presence rather than walls. It also challenges readers to consider how they provide shelter for others. Presence that protects becomes a refuge that strengthens.

When presence becomes shelter, it mirrors God's covering. It reflects His care through human hands and hearts. The safety created through faithful presence leaves an imprint that continues to comfort long after the moment has passed.

Because of her presence, safety was felt.

Because of her care, fear was eased.

Because of her sheltering presence, strength was restored.

Chapter 9 Reflection Page

Reflect

Shelter is often experienced through presence long before it is recognized. Take time to reflect on the spaces of safety in your life.

1. Who provided you with a sense of shelter during uncertain or difficult seasons?
   (Mother, caregiver, mentor, spiritual figure, or trusted presence.)

2. What actions, words, or behaviors helped you feel protected, understood, or at peace?

3. How did that sense of safety influence your confidence, healing, or ability to trust others?

____

____

____

Apply & Pray

Presence that shelters offers refuge without conditions.

4. In what ways can you intentionally create environments of safety and trust for others?

____

____

____

5. Are there areas of your life where you need to seek shelter—emotionally, spiritually, or relationally?

____

____

Prayer Prompt

Pause and rest in God's covering.

Lord, thank You for being my shelter and refuge. Thank You for the people whose presence provided safety in my life. Help me to reflect that same care and protection for others, creating spaces where trust, peace, and healing can grow. Amen.

Chapter 10

Loving Through Limitations

"And he said unto me, My grace is sufficient for thee: for my strength is made perfect in weakness."
— 2 Corinthians 12:9 (KJV)

Love is often imagined as limitless—endless energy, endless patience, endless capacity. Yet much of the love that shapes lives is offered within limitation. It is given through fatigue, restricted resources, unanswered prayers, and imperfect circumstances. Loving through limitation requires faith, humility, and grace.

Mothers and maternal figures frequently love within constraints they did not choose. Limited time, limited strength, limited support, and limited control over outcomes shape their daily decisions. Still, love persists. It adapts. It finds ways to show up even when conditions are less than ideal.

Paul's words in 2 Corinthians 12:9 remind us that limitation is not the absence of strength, but the space where grace operates most clearly. Weakness does not disqualify love; it refines it. God's grace fills the gaps human ability cannot.

Loving through limitation means showing care when energy is low and offering encouragement when answers are unclear. It means extending patience while navigating uncertainty and choosing presence even when perfection feels out of reach. This kind of love teaches resilience and realism.

Children often learn that love does not depend on ideal circumstances. They learn that commitment can exist alongside struggle and that care can be expressed without abundance. These lessons shape expectations and understanding later in life.

Limitation also invites creativity. When one path is blocked, love finds another. It may look like listening instead of fixing, praying instead of controlling, or remaining present instead of providing solutions. Love expressed this way carries depth and sincerity.

This chapter honors those who loved faithfully despite constraints—those who trusted God to supply what they could not. Their presence demonstrated that love does not require perfection, only willingness and trust.

For readers wrestling with their own limitations, this chapter offers reassurance. You do not need to have everything to give something meaningful. Grace meets you where you are and strengthens what you offer.

Because of her love, even within limits, care was felt. Because of her faith, grace filled the gaps. Because of her presence, love endured beyond circumstance.

Chapter 10 Reflection Page

Reflect

Love is often expressed most clearly within limitation. Take time to reflect on how grace has shown up in imperfect circumstances.

1. What limitations have shaped the way you give or receive love?
   (Time, energy, resources, health, support, or circumstances.)

2. How have those limitations influenced your understanding of grace, patience, or dependence on God?

3. Who in your life demonstrated love faithfully despite clear limitations?

____

____

____

Apply & Pray

Grace-filled love adapts rather than retreats.

4. In what areas of your life can you release the pressure to be perfect and trust God to work through your limitations?

____

____

____

5. How can you extend grace—to yourself or others—when limitations feel overwhelming?

____

____

Prayer Prompt

Pause and invite God's strength into your limitations.

Lord, thank You for meeting me where I am. Help me to trust that Your grace is sufficient, even when my strength feels small. Teach me to love faithfully within my limitations, knowing that You are at work through every imperfect offering. Amen.

Chapter 11

The Cost No One Applauds

"That thine alms may be in secret: and thy Father which seeth in secret himself shall reward thee openly."
— Matthew 6:4 (KJV)

Not all sacrifices are seen. Some of the greatest costs are paid quietly, without recognition, gratitude, or acknowledgment. They are absorbed in private moments and carried without complaint. This is the cost no one applauds.

Mothers and maternal figures often live in this space. They give time that could have been used for rest, energy that could have been reserved for themselves, and resources that stretch beyond comfort. Much of this giving happens unnoticed, folded into daily routines and silent decisions.

Jesus' words in Matthew 6:4 affirm the value of unseen faithfulness. God sees what is done in secret. He honors obedience that is not performed for recognition. This promise brings comfort to those whose sacrifices remain invisible to others.

The cost no one applauds includes emotional labor—listening when tired, encouraging when discouraged, and remaining steady when overwhelmed. It includes choosing restraint, patience, and grace in moments that test resolve. These sacrifices may not be acknowledged publicly, but they shape lives profoundly.

Over time, the weight of unseen sacrifice can feel heavy. When appreciation is delayed or absent, weariness may set in. Yet faithfulness continues, anchored in purpose rather than praise. This kind of endurance reflects trust in God rather than reliance on human validation.

Many only recognize these costs later in life. What once seemed effortless is revealed as intentional sacrifice. What appeared routine is understood as commitment. Gratitude often grows with maturity and reflection.

This chapter invites readers to acknowledge both the sacrifices made on their behalf and the ones they themselves have carried quietly. Recognition—even if internal—creates space for healing and gratitude. It also reminds us to extend appreciation while there is still time.

Faithfulness without applause builds character. It teaches humility, perseverance, and reliance on God's reward rather than public recognition. Presence expressed this way speaks loudly, even in silence.

Because of her sacrifice, needs were met.
Because of her obedience, stability was maintained.
Because of her faithfulness, impact was made without applause.

Chapter 11 Reflection Page

Reflect

Some sacrifices shape lives without ever being acknowledged. Take time to reflect on what was given quietly and faithfully.

1. Who made sacrifices for you that were rarely seen or publicly recognized?
   (Time, energy, emotional labor, prayer, or personal dreams set aside.)

2. What sacrifices do you now recognize as having a lasting impact on your life or direction?

3. How does acknowledging those sacrifices change your perspective today?

____

____

Apply & Pray

Faithfulness offered without applause still carries eternal value.

4. In what areas of your life are you currently giving or sacrificing without recognition?

____

____

____

5. How can you release the need for validation and trust God to honor your faithfulness in His timing?

____

____

____

Prayer Prompt

Pause and place unseen sacrifices in God's care.

Lord, You see what others may overlook. Thank You for honoring faithfulness that is carried quietly and given without applause. Help me to trust that nothing offered in love and obedience is wasted. Teach me to give with humility and to rest in Your reward. Amen.

Chapter 12

Seeds That Take Time to Grow

"In the morning sow thy seed, and in the evening withhold not thine hand: for thou knowest not whether shall prosper, either this or that, or whether they both shall be alike good."
— Ecclesiastes 11:6 (KJV)

Not every seed shows immediate results. Some require time beneath the surface before any visible growth appears. Faithfulness often involves sowing without certainty, trusting that what is planted will one day bear fruit. This truth is especially evident in the influence of a mother's presence.

Mothers and maternal figures sow seeds daily—through instruction, example, prayer, correction, encouragement, and love. These seeds are planted consistently, often without assurance of when or how they will take root. Much of this sowing happens quietly, with no guarantee of immediate return.

Ecclesiastes 11:6 speaks to the discipline of continual sowing. It acknowledges uncertainty while encouraging persistence. The verse does not promise instant harvest; it calls for faithfulness. Growth is not always visible, but planting must continue.

Many seeds planted in childhood do not surface until much later. Values resurface in adulthood. Faith reemerges in difficult seasons. Lessons once ignored gain meaning with maturity. What seemed forgotten was never lost—it was growing unseen.

This chapter honors the patience required to sow without rushing the outcome. Mothers often trust God with results they may never fully witness. They release control while remaining committed, believing that their presence is doing work beyond their sight.

Waiting can be difficult. Delayed fruit may tempt discouragement. Yet faithfulness remains rooted in trust rather than outcome. Seeds planted with love and consistency are never wasted, even when growth appears slow.

For readers reflecting on their own lives, this chapter invites recognition of seeds planted long ago. It encourages gratitude for the patient sowing that shaped direction, character, and faith. It also challenges readers to continue sowing in their own spheres of influence.

Presence that sows patiently reflects confidence in God's timing. It understands that growth unfolds according to divine order, not human schedules. What is planted in faith will emerge in season.

Because of her patience, seeds were planted.
Because of her faithfulness, growth was nurtured unseen.
Because of her presence, harvest came in its time.

Chapter 12 Reflection page

Reflect

Not all growth is immediate. Many seeds are planted long before they are seen. Take time to reflect on the seeds that were sown in your life.

1. What values, lessons, or beliefs were planted in you that only became meaningful later in life?

2. Who consistently sowed into your life, even when results were not visible?

3. How has time revealed the importance of seeds that once seemed unnoticed?

Apply & Pray

Faithful sowing requires patience and trust in God's timing.

4. In what areas of your life are you currently sowing seeds without seeing immediate results?

5. How can you remain faithful in planting, trusting God with the timing and outcome?

Prayer Prompt

Pause and entrust both planting and harvest to God.

Lord, thank You for the seeds planted in my life through faithful presence. Help me to trust Your timing when growth feels delayed. Strengthen my faith to continue sowing with patience, knowing that You bring the increase in due season. Amen.

Chapter 13

Still Speaking After the Moment Has Passed

"Give her of the fruit of her hands; and let her own works praise her in the gates."
— **Proverbs 31:31 (KJV)**

Presence does not end when a moment passes. It continues—through memory, influence, values, and faith. Long after words have faded and circumstances have changed, presence still speaks.

Many do not realize the full impact of a mother's presence until distance, time, or transition creates perspective. What once felt ordinary is later understood as intentional. What once felt constant is later recognized as foundational. Presence reveals its voice most clearly in hindsight.

The work of a mother is rarely finished in the moment. Its fruit unfolds over time. Values surface in decisions. Faith reappears in difficult seasons. Lessons return when guidance is needed most. The echo of presence continues to shape lives quietly and faithfully.

Proverbs 31:31 reminds us that a woman's works speak for themselves. Recognition does not always come through ceremony or applause, but through lived evidence. Her influence is seen in the lives she touched, the stability she helped create, and the faith she modeled consistently.

Presence still speaks in the way someone loves, leads, forgives, and perseveres. It speaks when compassion is chosen over convenience. It speaks when faith is practiced without performance. It speaks when values once taught are lived out in new generations.

This chapter honors the truth that legacy is not limited to proximity. Even when physical presence changes—through distance, transition, or loss—the influence remains. Presence outlives the moment because it was never confined to it.

For some readers, this chapter brings comfort. It affirms that what was given mattered and still matters. For others, it brings responsibility—a reminder that presence continues through how we live and what we pass on.

The voice of presence does not demand attention. It does not announce itself loudly. It speaks through character, consistency, and choices made long after instruction has ended. It speaks through faith that endures and love that remains steady.

As this book closes, it invites reflection not only on what was received, but on what will be continued. Presence is a gift that does not expire. It becomes a legacy carried forward through intentional living.

Her presence still speaks—in the lives she shaped.
Her presence still speaks—in the faith she modeled.
Her presence still speaks—long after the moment has passed

Final Reflection page

Look Back

As this journey comes to a close, take time to reflect on the presence that shaped your life and continues to speak today.

1. Whose presence has continued to influence you long after the moment, season, or relationship changed?

2. What lessons, values, or faith practices still guide your decisions today because of her presence?

3. In what ways do you now see her influence showing up in your words, choices, or character?

Carry It Forward

Presence does not end—it continues through how we live.

4. What parts of her presence do you want to intentionally carry forward in your own life?

5. Who might experience the echo of her presence through you in the days ahead?

Closing Prayer Prompt

Pause and offer gratitude, remembrance, and commitment.

Lord, thank You for the presence that shaped me and continues to speak into my life. Help me to honor that legacy by how I live, love, and lead. May what was poured into me not end with me, but continue through faithful presence, grace, and purpose. Amen.

Closing Reflection

As these pages come to an end, the work of presence does not.

What you have reflected on—what was given, carried, taught, protected, and sown—was never meant to stop with remembrance alone. Presence continues through how we live, love, forgive, and show up for others. The influence that shaped you now finds expression through you.

Some of what was poured into your life may have gone unnoticed at the time. Some sacrifices may only now be fully understood. Yet nothing given in love was wasted. Every prayer, correction, quiet strength, and faithful act contributed to a legacy that still speaks.

This book honored the presence that shaped you.
The next journey is about the presence you offer.

Your Presence Matters is not a departure from this story—it is its continuation. It is an invitation to live intentionally, to recognize that the way you show up carries weight, and to understand that your consistency, faith, and love have influence beyond what you can see.

This book was never about perfection. It was about faithfulness. It was about staying when it mattered, loving through limits, and trusting God with seeds that required time to grow. It was about presence that sheltered, guided, and endured.

As you move forward, carry what was given with intention. Let gratitude shape your remembrance and purpose guide your presence. Whether you are honoring the influence of a mother, becoming a source of stability for others, or continuing a legacy of faith, know this truth:

Her presence still speaks.

And now—**your presence matters.**

Closing Prayer

Lord, thank You for the presence that shaped my life. Thank You for the love that stayed, the faith that endured, and the sacrifices that were carried quietly.

As I move forward, help me to recognize that my presence matters. Teach me to show up with intention, wisdom, and grace. Let the influence poured into me be reflected through how I love, serve, and lead others.

Where healing is needed, bring restoration. Where gratitude is overdue, soften my heart. Where responsibility is calling, strengthen my resolve.

May what was given not end with me. Let it continue through faithful presence, purposeful living, and a legacy that honors You. In every season ahead, remind me that presence still speaks—and that my presence matters. Amen.

About the Author

Ethan L. Ketterer is an author, speaker, and reflective voice committed to honoring faith, presence, and the unseen influences that shape lives. Through his writing, he explores themes of legacy, endurance, identity, and the quiet strength found in faithful living.

Ethan's work is rooted in a deep appreciation for the impact of consistent presence—particularly the influence of mothers and maternal figures whose sacrifices, faith, and love often go unrecognized. His writing invites readers to slow down, reflect, and acknowledge the moments and people that have shaped them long after the moment has passed.

As the founder of **KTURN**, a purpose-driven platform focused on motivation, inspiration, encouragement, and empowerment, Ethan creates books and resources designed to foster growth, healing, and intentional living. His work is used in personal reflection, group study, conferences, and community settings.

Her Presence Still Speaks is a continuation of Ethan's commitment to honoring legacy and encouraging readers to carry forward what was poured into them—through presence, faith, and purposeful living.